edexcel
w

Crisis

29/32

Crisis is a national charity for single homeless people. They want to raise their profile by posting cardbo collecting boxes into every home in the UK.

You are asked to design a card collecting box which will help to raise their profile. The box must be cap of folding flat for easy storage.

Marks will be awarded for:

A creative solution which clearly promotes the charity
Details of materials and construction
Surface graphics and use of colour
Details of how the box will fold flat

IDEA = 6 MARKS
= 5 MARKS
= 5 MARKS
= 4 MARKS

Below, draw a 3D view of your collection box, adding notes and/or sketches to explain how it folds flat.

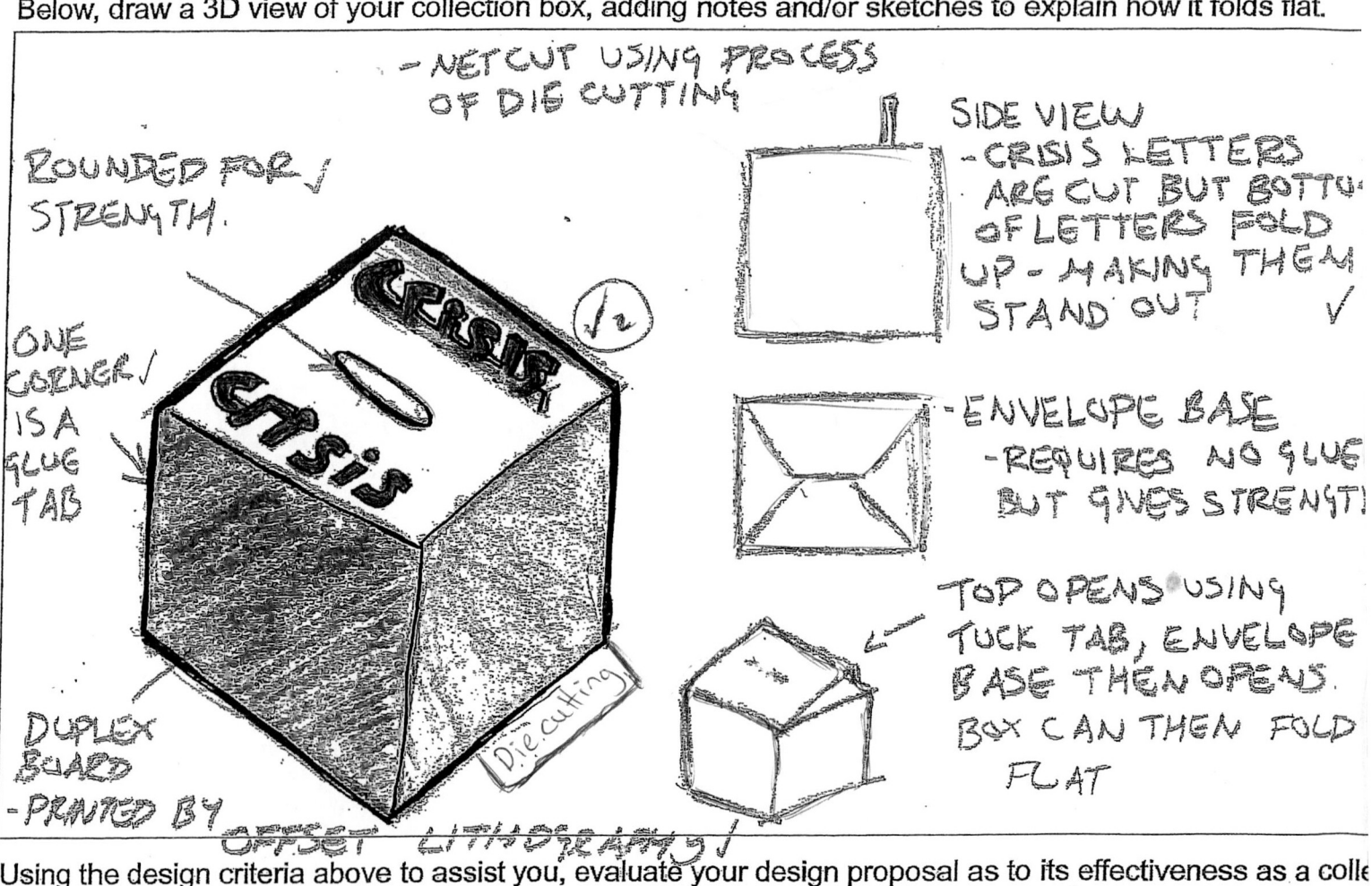

- NET CUT USING PROCESS OF DIE CUTTING

ROUNDED FOR STRENGTH.

ONE CORNER IS A GLUE TAB

DUPLEX BOARD
- PRINTED BY OFFSET LITHOGRAPHY

Die cutting

SIDE VIEW
- CRISIS LETTERS ARE CUT BUT BOTTO OF LETTERS FOLD UP - MAKING THEM STAND OUT

- ENVELOPE BASE
- REQUIRES NO GLUE BUT GIVES STRENGT!

TOP OPENS USING TUCK TAB, ENVELOPE BASE THEN OPENS. BOX CAN THEN FOLD FLAT

Using the design criteria above to assist you, evaluate your design proposal as to its effectiveness as a colle

- Box must fold flat - The minimal use of glue on the corner glue tab alle also allows the box to carry a relatively large amount of weight (appro
- Must be bold + stand out ✓ - Simple Bold /Bright colours used
- Must be relatively cheap to manufacture ✓ - The box using quite a sm manufacturing costs ✓ - also the products manufacturing costs are

Complete the table showing important criteria for your collection box and give your reasons.
An example has been provided.

Design criteria	Reasons
The box must fold flat	This will reduce storage space and make it easier to transport the boxes from the printers to the charity
Must be bold and 'stand out'. /10	So it attracts the customers attention leading to a greater chance of a donation. /10
Must be relatively cheap to manufacture. /10	The less money spent on manufacturing costs will lead to lower 'overheads'. - have more possibility to make profit. /10

- logo - out of card

In the space below draw the net for your collection box.

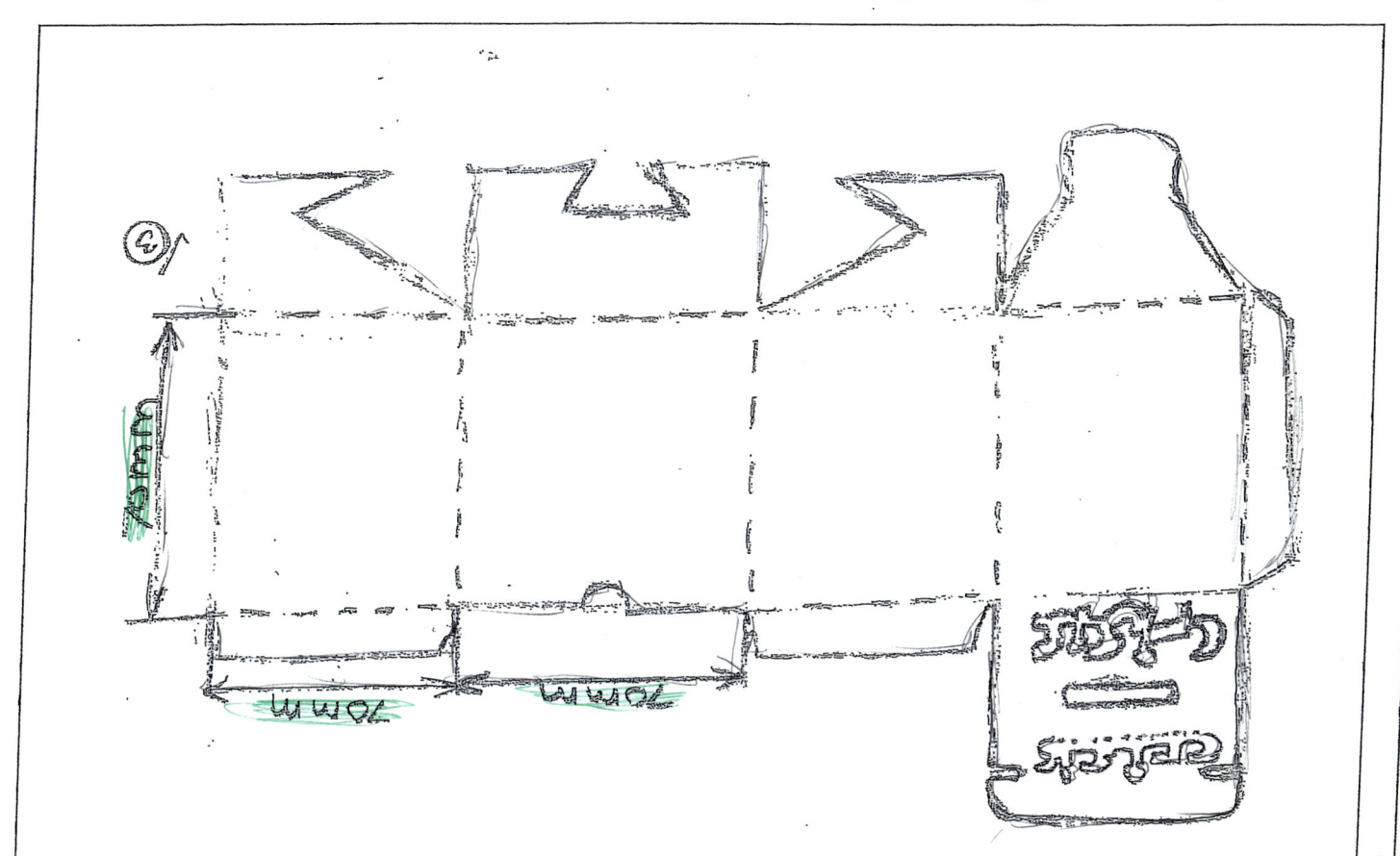

[Net drawing with dimensions 70mm and 70mm, labelled "Asthma", with logo "charity" shown]

/10

...ction box as well as a promotional product

...s the box to be disassembled, laid flat, the envelope been...

x 1kg)
6 marks
- These will potentially attract the donators.
...ll amount of card and minimal glue. Hardy reducing...
...owered by using a reduced amount of ink colours + is only

⑤

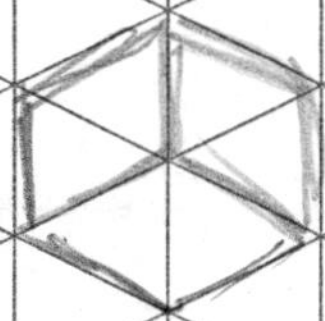

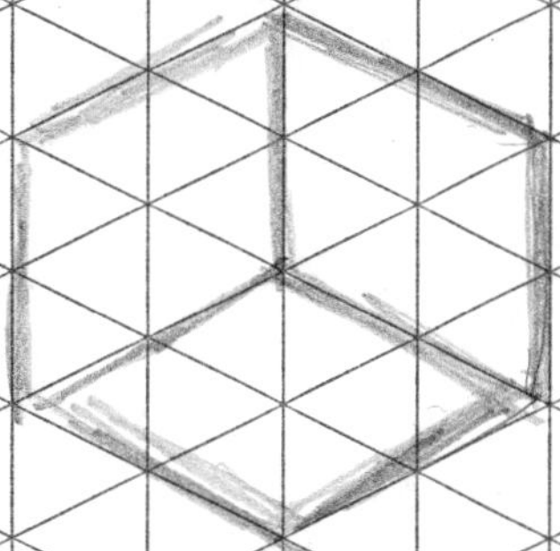

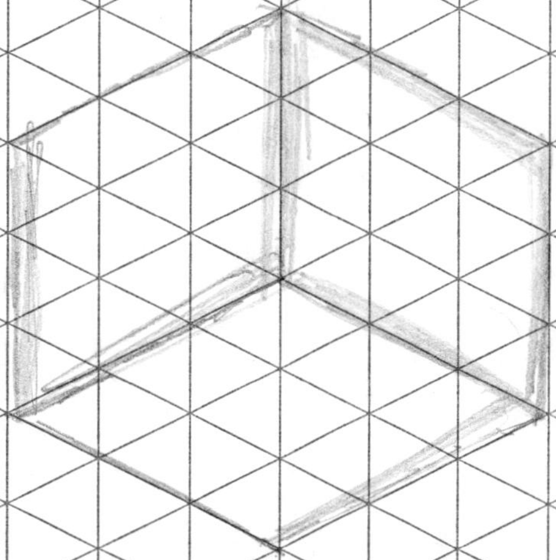

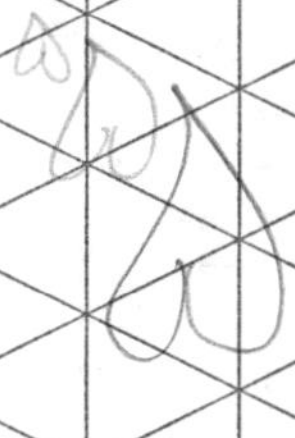

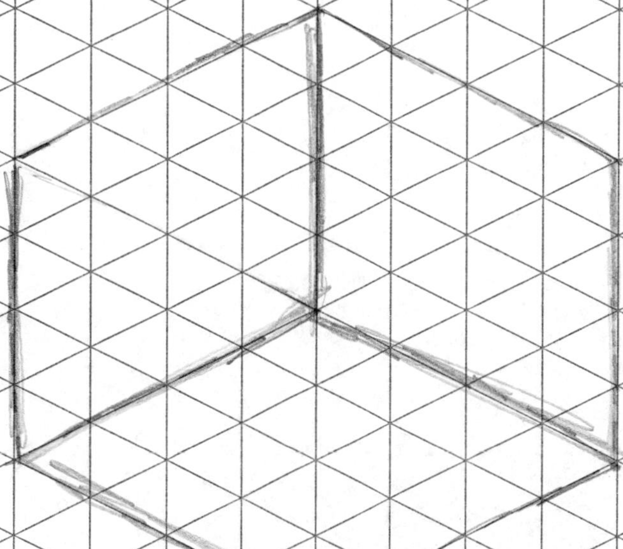

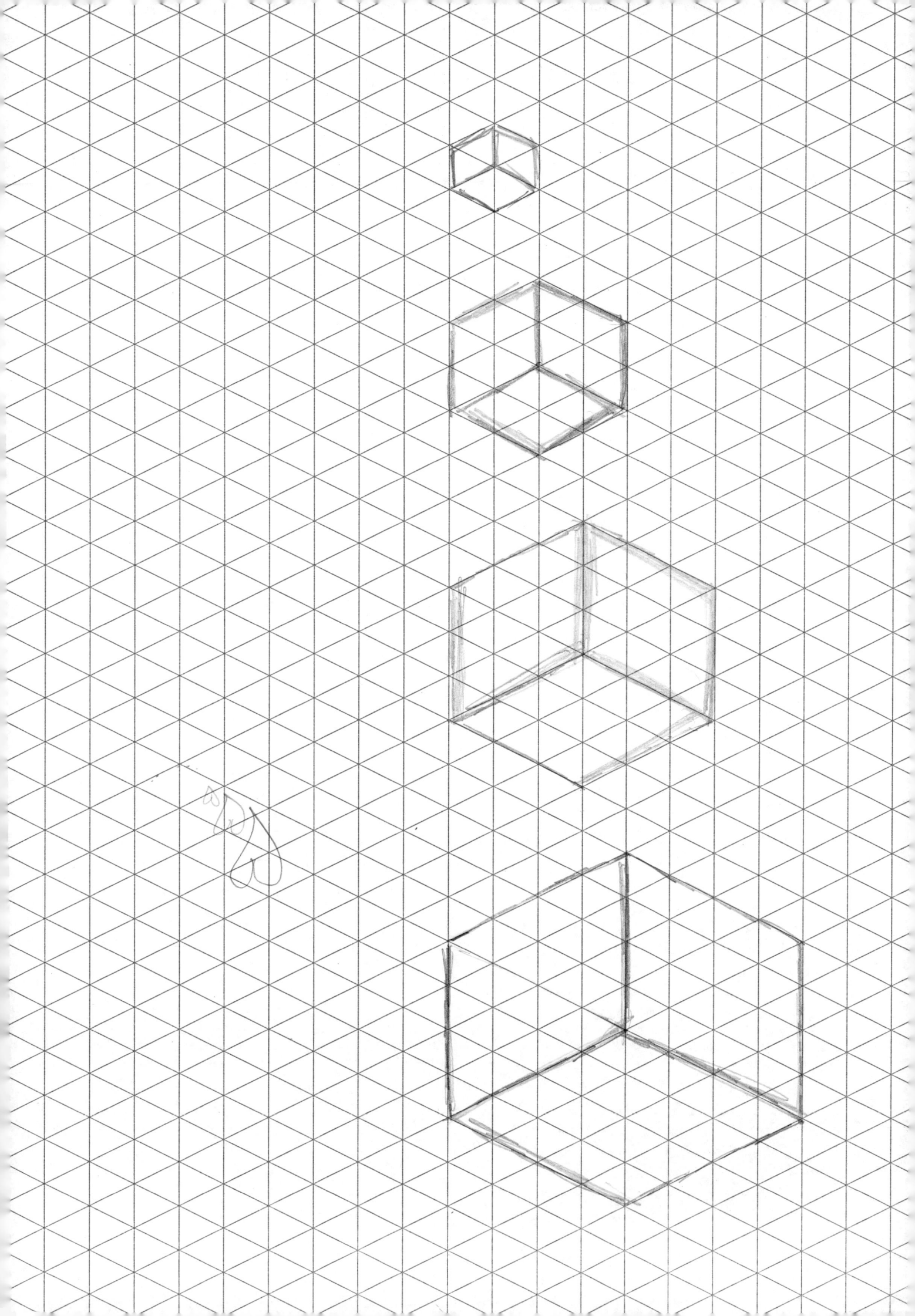

It's another Quality Book from CGP

This book is for anyone doing AQA GCSE Product Design.

It contains lots of tricky questions just like the ones that could come up in the exam. They're designed to make you sweat — because that's the only way you'll get any better.

It's also got a few daft bits in to try and make the whole experience at least vaguely entertaining for you.

What CGP is all about

Our sole aim here at CGP is to produce the highest quality books — carefully written, immaculately presented and dangerously close to being funny.

Then we work our socks off to get them out to you — at the cheapest possible prices.

Contents

Exam Advice 1

Section One — The Design Process

Evolution of Product Design 4
Human Factors in Design 6
Research and Specifications 7
Design Methods and Influences 9
Practical Design and Modelling 10
Presenting and Protecting Design Ideas 11
Working Schedules and Quality Control 12

Section Two — Graphical Techniques

Drawing Techniques 14
Drawing Enhancements 18
Presentation Techniques 20

Section Three — Packaging and Marketing

Packaging and the Environment 22
Labelling 24
Brands and Marketing 26

Section Four — Materials and Components

Properties of Materials 27
Paper and Card 28
Timber 30
Manufactured Boards 32
Metals 34
Plastics 36
Ceramics 38
Textiles 40
Food 43
Electrical Components 46
Mechanical Components 48
Fixings and Bindings 50
Standard Components 51
New Materials 52

Section Five — Social and Environmental Issues

Safety 54
Quality 56
Ethics and Environmental Issues 58

Section Six — Processes and Manufacture

Tools 61
Forming and Bending 63
Casting and Moulding 65
Scale of Production 67
Manufacturing Systems and ICT 69
Manufacturing Systems 71
CAD/CAM 73
Consistency of Production 75

Published by CGP

Editors:
Katie Braid, Rosie Gillham, Heather Gregson, Murray Hamilton,
Adam Moorhouse, Caley Simpson, Jane Towle.

Contributors:
Catherine Atsiaris, Ryan Ball, Charlotte Esposito,
Phil Holton, Debbie McGrory.

With thanks to Ryan Ball for the content review.
With thanks to Sharon Keeley, Katie Braid and Paul Anderson for the proofreading.

With thanks to Laura Stoney for the copyright research.

ISBN: 978 1 84762 390 4

Clipart from Corel®

With thanks to iStockphoto® for permission to use the ATM picture on page 6, and the concrete picture on page 39.

With thanks to BSI for permission to reproduce the Kitemark symbol on page 24. Kitemark and the Kitemark symbol are registered trademarks of BSI. For more information visit www.kitemark.com.

Printed by Elanders Ltd, Newcastle upon Tyne.

Based on the classic CGP style created by Richard Parsons.

Text, design, layout and original illustrations © Coordination Group Publications Ltd. (CGP) 2009
All rights reserved.

Photocopying more than one chapter of this book is not permitted. Extra copies are available from CGP.
0800 1712 712 • www.cgpbooks.co.uk

Exam Advice

The Exam Paper is in Two Sections

1) There's just one exam for AQA Product Design, but it's split into two sections — Section A and B.
2) You need to answer all of the questions in both sections.

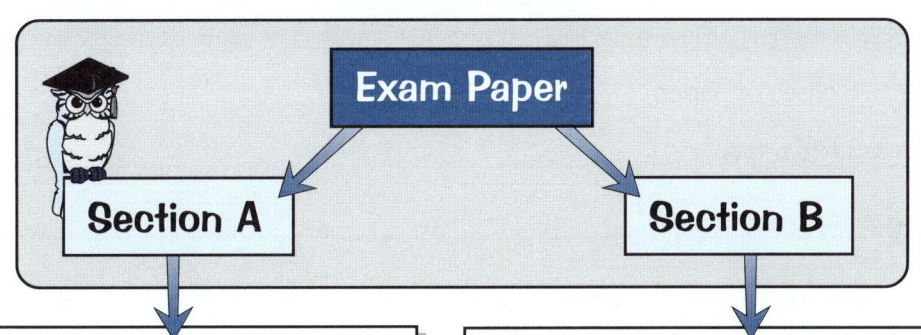

```
                        Exam Paper
                       /          \
                  Section A     Section B
```

Section A is the design question. The questions in Section A will all be on the same theme, e.g. products related to sports. You'll be asked to develop a design idea — it's the place in the exam for showing that you can come up with original and creative ideas.

Section B covers everything you've learnt about in your Product Design course — materials, tools, how to design things, how to make things, health and safety, environmental issues... There'll be a mixture of short and longer answer questions, as well as some sketching and some tables to fill in.

A little while before the exam, your teacher will give you a Preparation Sheet. This gives you the theme of the Section A question — use it to do some research.

3) The exam lasts for 2 hours. Each question will have a suggestion of how long you should spend on it. Try to follow this — it really will help you to have a good go at every question.
4) Some of your answers will be assessed for quality of written communication — that's spelling, punctuation and grammar, as well as how clear your answer is. You'll be told which question this is on the front of the exam paper — so read all that information carefully and put a note to yourself next to the relevant question.

There are a Few Golden Rules

1) Always, always, always make sure you read the question properly. For example, if the question asks you to name three products, make sure you name three, otherwise you could miss out on marks.
2) If you're asked to add notes or annotate a sketch don't just add labels — you need to explain your ideas fully.
3) It's a good idea to underline the important bits of the question. Then you can keep checking to make sure you're not going off track and waffling about stuff that's not going to get you any marks.
4) Pay attention to the number of marks a question is worth — if it's worth three marks, give three good points. And try to fill most of the space available for the answer. If there are three lines and you've only filled one, you probably haven't written enough.
5) Always use the right technical words — words like 'tone' and 'ergonomic' make examiners happy.
6) Make your answers as specific as possible. If you're asked to suggest a material, don't just write card — give a specific type of card, e.g. corrugated board.

Exam Advice

Exam Advice

You Need to Understand the Command Words

Command words are the words in a question that tell you what to do — describe, explain, etc. If you don't know what they mean, you won't be able to answer the questions properly. Boo hoo.

Name...
If you're asked to name something just say what it's called — you don't need to give any extra information.

6 a) Name two types of paper.

  1. cartridge paper

  2. grid paper

(2 marks)

Identify / State / Give...
You just need to write down the answer — you don't need to explain it.

2 Identify a target market for the following products.

  a) A poster advertising a new doll.

  parents of young girls

(1 mark)

Choose...
In Product Design, not everyone will have studied all the material groups — for example, you may have studied textiles but not food or wood. So if you're asked to choose, choose to answer the ones that you have learnt about.

4 Choose a material from the box and name a product it could be used to make.

| PVC | MDF | Cheese | LYCRA® | Duplex board | China Clay | Aluminium |

Material LYCRA®   Product Leotard

(1 mark)

Describe...
Describing means picking out the features — of, say, an object or a process. If you're asked to just 'briefly describe' something you don't need to go into too much detail.

4 Describe the process of producing paper from trees.

Trees are cut down and the bark is stripped off. The wood is cut into small pieces and heated and treated with chemicals to form a pulp. The pulp is then washed and bleached. It's then pressed flat by rollers and cut to size.

(4 marks)

Exam Advice

Explain...

If you're asked to explain something, you need to give reasons — don't just write out what it is.

3 b) Explain why manufacturers use standard components

Standard components are used because they're cheap so they save manufacturers money. They also save time, so manufacture is more efficient.

(2 marks)

Evaluate...

You need to weigh something up — here you need to look at your idea and the specification and decide whether your idea has covered each point.

1 b) A design specification for a children's book has the following points:
- The book must be suitable for a young child.
- The book must be made from environmentally friendly material.

Evaluate your design idea against the design specification above.

Analyse is similar to evaluate — you need to pick out and evaluate the features of something.

The bright colours will appeal to children, and the large font size will make it easy for them to read. The book will be made from recycled paper so it will be environmentally friendly, as trees won't need to be felled to make new paper.

(4 marks)

Compare / Contrast...

You need to talk about the differences between two things. Use words like whereas and but.

7 Compare the finishing methods of painting and lacquering for a metal product.

Painting and lacquering both involve coating the metal product to protect it. But lacquering gives a transparent coating so you can still see the metal, whereas painting leaves the metal covered so that it can't be seen.

(3 marks)

Discuss...

When you discuss something you need to look at it from both sides — for example, by giving its advantages and disadvantages.

5 Discuss the issues related to the use of plastic in packaging.

Plastic is often used for packaging because it is cheap and durable. However, most plastic is made using crude oil, which is a finite resource. Also, plastic is often disposed of in landfill, which can be bad for the environment.

(3 marks)

Section One — The Design Process

Evolution of Product Design — 1

1 The design of products has evolved because of **technology push** and **market pull**.

a) Describe what the terms technology push and market pull mean.

Technology push: *It is about what manufacturers can provide.*
....
(1 mark)

Market pull: *It is about consumers want.*
....
(1 mark)

b) **Two different** types of computer are shown below.

Laptop   **Base computer**

i) Identify and explain **one** difference between the computers that is likely to have been caused by **technology push**.

....
....
(2 marks)

ii) Identify and explain **one** difference between the computers that is likely to have been caused by **market pull**.

....
....
(2 marks)

c) Besides technology pull and market push, describe **another factor** that might cause the design of a computer to evolve. Explain how the computer might change in response to it.

....
....
(2 marks)

2 Manufacturers are always working towards **continuous improvement**.

Explain why they work towards continuous improvement.

They would work towards continuous improvement to earn much more money. Also so their products are as good as possible.
(2 marks)

Section 1 — The Design Process

Evolution of Product Design — 2

3   A variety of **design movements** can influence product development.

a)   In the space below, sketch a design for a product in the **Art Deco** style.
Your product can be a chair, a cushion or some wallpaper.

Annotate your sketch to explain how it has been influenced by the Art Deco movement.

Product: ....

Using some colour can get you a mark in design questions.

(4 marks)

b)   Describe the key features of **two** of the following design movements.
Circle the **two** movements you describe.

Design Movement	Features
Arts and Crafts	Based on patterns found in nature.
Bauhaus	Chrome tubing and black leather.
De Stijl	Basic, with simple shapes, vertical and horizontal lines.
Postmodernist	Bright, contrasting colours and different materials.
Arts and Crafts	Furniture in this style is upright and angular.
Bauhaus	Founded by Walter Gropius.
De Stijl	Gerrit Rietveld's Red and Blue chair is a De Stijl design.
Postmodernist	They include kitsch ('tacky and tasteless') and extreme minimalism.

(6 marks)

Section 1 — The Design Process

Human Factors in Design

1 Products are designed to be suitable for 90% of the **target market** to use.

    a) Suggest **two** groups of people that may find it difficult to use the cash machine shown opposite. Give a reason for each answer.

    Group 1: ....

    Reason: ....

    ....
    (2 marks)

    Group 2: ....

    Reason: ....

    ....
    (2 marks)

    b) Explain how the design of the cash machine could be altered to make it suitable for these **two** groups.

    Group 1: ....
    (1 mark)

    Group 2: ....
    (1 mark)

2 It's important to consider **ergonomics** when designing a new product.

    a) Explain what the term 'ergonomics' means.

    ....
    (1 mark)

    b) Explain why ergonomics is important in design.

    ....

    ....
    (2 marks)

3 Manufacturers make tennis rackets using **anthropometric data**.

    a) What is anthropometric data?

    ....
    (1 mark)

    b) Explain **two** ways that anthropometric data could be useful when designing a tennis racket.

    1. ....

    2. ....
    (2 marks)

Section 1 — The Design Process

Research and Specifications — 1

1 The **design brief** is an important part of the design process.

  a) What is a design brief?

  ....
  (1 mark)

  b) What should a design brief include?

  ....

  ....
  (2 marks)

2 A manufacturer wants to design a **portable** holder for computer games.

  a) Explain why the designer should carry out some research before starting the project.

  ....

  ....
  (2 marks)

  b) The results of a market research questionnaire are shown below.

   i) Describe how these findings would affect the design of the product.

   ....

   ....

   ....

   ....

Results of Market Research
Average number of hours spent on computer = 12
Average number of computer games owned = 15
Most common size of computer game = 19 cm × 14 cm

   (2 marks)

   ii) Suggest **two** other questions that it would be sensible to ask during market research.

   1. ....

   2. ....
   (2 marks)

  c) **i)** Designers use product analysis during research. Describe what product analysis involves.

   ....
   (1 mark)

   ii) List **two** pieces of information you can find out from product analysis.

   1. ....

   2. ....
   (2 marks)

Section 1 — The Design Process

Research and Specifications — 2

3 You have been asked to design a wall calendar for a target group of **your choice**.

Identify **two** design criteria for your target group.
Give a reason for each design criteria.

Target Group: ....

Design Criteria 1: ....

....

Design Criteria 2: ....

....

(4 marks)

4 Identify **three** design criteria used to create the children's birthday card shown below.
Give a reason for each criteria. An example is given for you.

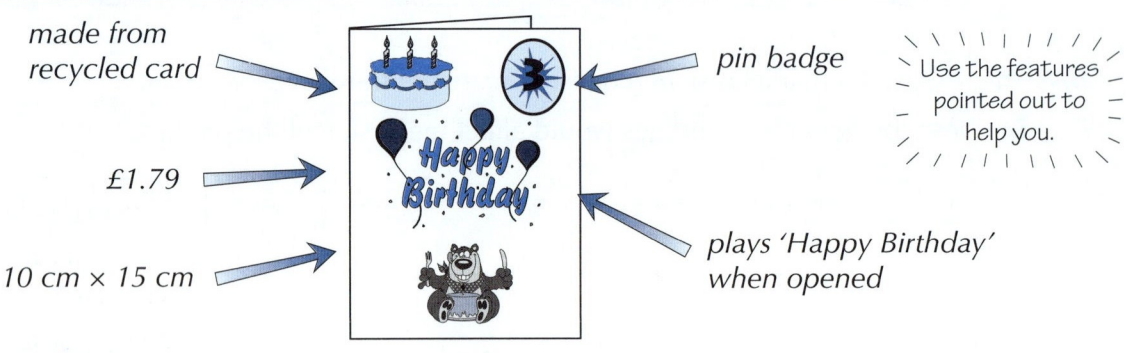

- made from recycled card
- £1.79
- 10 cm × 15 cm
- pin badge
- plays 'Happy Birthday' when opened

Use the features pointed out to help you.

Design Criteria	Reason
It must have bright colours.	*The card should use bright, bold colours so that it appeals to young children.*

(6 marks)

Section 1 — The Design Process

Design Methods and Influences

1 Nature can be a **design inspiration** for the structure, function or aesthetics of a product.

In the space below, design a container you can drink from using nature as an inspiration. Annotate your sketch to explain how nature has been used in its design.

Think about how nature could inspire the colour, texture and shape of the product.

Dave always found inspiration in nature

(4 marks)

2 Colours, textures and finishes are often used to represent **moods** and **feelings**.

a) Suggest a **colour** for a winter scarf and give a reason for your choice.

Colour: ....

Reason: ....

....

(2 marks)

b) Suggest a **finish** for the microwave and give a reason for your choice.

Finish: ....

Reason: ....

....

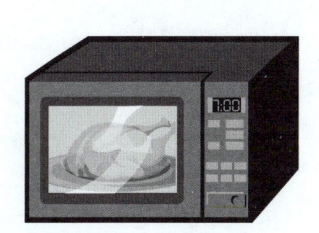

(2 marks)

Section 1 — The Design Process

Practical Design and Modelling

1 A company is designing a new milk carton aimed at **young children**. A sketch of the new carton is shown below.

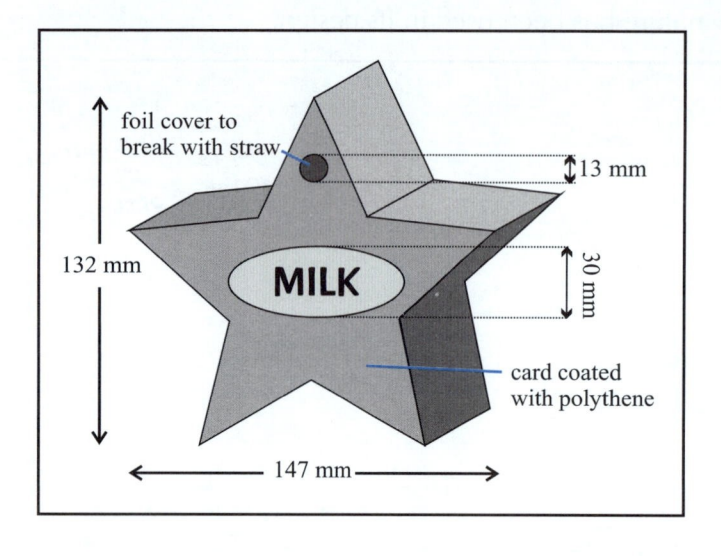

[Sketch of star-shaped milk carton with labels: "foil cover to break with straw", "13 mm", "132 mm", "30 mm", "MILK", "card coated with polythene", "147 mm"]

a) Identify **one** part of the carton that would need to be measured very **accurately** and explain why.

Part: ....

....

Reason: ....

....

....

....

(2 marks)

b) Explain how modelling can improve the design of products.

....

....

(2 marks)

c) Describe how CAD can be used in the modelling process.

....

....

(2 marks)

d) The company wants to mass produce their new carton. Evaluate how suitable their design is for mass production.

....

....

....

....

(4 marks)

e) Explain why prototypes are useful in the design process.

....

....

(2 marks)

Section 1 — The Design Process

Presenting and Protecting Design Ideas

1 At the end of the design process the final design is **presented** to the client.

   a) Name and describe **two** types of presentation drawing.

   1. ....

   ....

   2. ....

   ....
   (4 marks)

   b) Describe **two** benefits of using CAD to present ideas to clients.

   1. ....

   2. ....
   (2 marks)

2 Chatteraway Ltd. has finalised the designs of **two new** mobile phones, the zoomFone and the Super-sonicFone. Details of the designs are shown below.

zoomFone
- Unique streamlined shape
- Screen
- Number pad

Super-sonicFone
- Sonic sensing panel. This revolutionary new technology allows the phone to adjust its ring volume depending on the level of noise in the room.
- Screen
- Number pad

   a) Name the kind of legal protection Chatteraway Ltd. could use to protect the design of the **zoomFone**. Give a reason for your answer.

   Copyright is good for protecting ideas, but other forms of legal protection are better for protecting designs and technologies.

   Name: ....

   Reason: ....

   ....
   (3 marks)

   b) Name the kind of legal protection Chatteraway Ltd. could use to protect the **Super-sonicFone**. Give a reason for your answer.

   Name: ....

   Reason: ....

   ....
   (3 marks)

Section 1 — The Design Process

Working Schedules and Quality Control — 1

1 Quality control checks are an important part of any **quality assurance system**.

    a) Explain the purpose of quality control checks.

        ....

        (1 mark)

    b) Describe **two** other features of a good quality assurance system.

        1. ....

        2. ....

        (2 marks)

2 A company has started producing red, leather recliner sofas.

    Suggest **three** features that may be checked as part of quality control.

    1. ....

    2. ....

    3. ....

    (3 marks)

3 Components are usually checked for size before products are assembled. The **tolerances** for the components of a kitchen knife are shown below.

80 mm (± 1.5)   150 mm (± 2)

    a) **i)** Give the largest and smallest length that would be acceptable for the blade of the knife.

        Largest: ....

        Smallest: ....

        (2 marks)

    ii) The handle of a kitchen knife measures 81.4 mm. State whether the handle would pass the length quality control check. Give a reason for your answer.

        ....

        ....

        (2 marks)

    b) Identify **one** other characteristic of the knife that might be tested during quality control checks.

        ....

        (1 mark)

Section 1 — The Design Process

Working Schedules and Quality Control — 2

4 Companies use **production plans** to plan the making of their products.

a) Give **two** features which should be included in a production plan.

1. ....

2. ....
(2 marks)

b) Suggest **two** ways that a manufacturer could present a production plan.

1. ....

2. ....
(2 marks)

5 Your school is going to produce a batch of musical badges to sell at the school music concert. The badges can be made in **four steps**, shown below.

1. Cut out the main shape.
2. Finish the edges with a file.
3. Stick the music device and safety pin onto the back with adhesive.
4. Paint a design on the front.

In the space below, draw a **flow chart** showing the work order for making a badge. Include **two** quality control checks in your flow chart.

(4 marks)

Section 1 — The Design Process

Section Two — Graphical Techniques

Drawing Techniques — 1

1 A client needs a **logo** for a new fruit cereal bar for children. It must include appropriate images and the name 'Fruit Fun'.

Remember — annotate means add notes.

Sketch and annotate **two** design ideas in the space below.

Using some colour can get you a mark in design questions.

(8 marks)

2 **Isometric drawing** is one way to present designs.

a) Give **two advantages** of isometric drawings.

1. ....

2. ....

(2 marks)

b) Use the isometric grid below to produce a **wireframe** drawing of a box 30 mm wide, 40 mm deep and 20 mm high.

10 mm

(4 marks)

Section 2 — Graphical Techniques

Drawing Techniques — 2

3 The bookcase on the right needs to be assembled at home by the consumer. **Instructions** are needed to help the consumer assemble it.

a) Name the style of drawing that would be most suitable for the instructions. Explain why this style of drawing is suitable.

Name: ....

Explanation: ....

....

(2 marks)

b) Draw assembly instructions for the bookcase using this style of drawing.

(3 marks)

4 A point of sale display unit is shown below.

Make a **sectional drawing** by cutting vertically through the line XY.

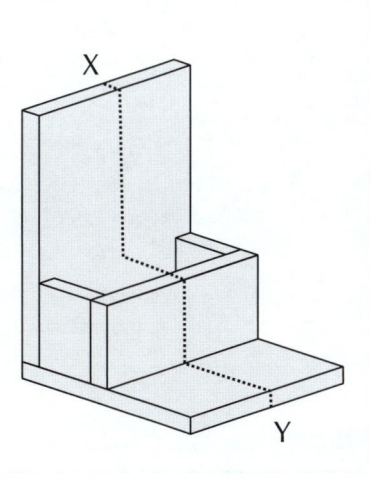

(2 marks)

Section 2 — Graphical Techniques

Drawing Techniques — 3

5 **Perspective drawing** is one type of three-dimensional drawing.

a) Give **one advantage** of drawing in perspective.

....

(1 mark)

b) The picture below shows a design for a tissue box.

Make a **one-point perspective** drawing of the tissue box.

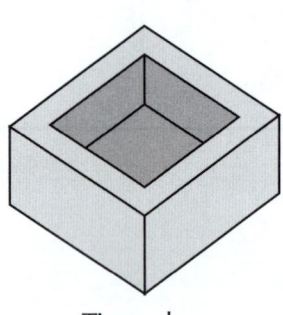

Tissue box

(2 marks)

c) Using **two-point perspective**, redraw the lamp shade shown below as it would look if it was **above the horizon**.

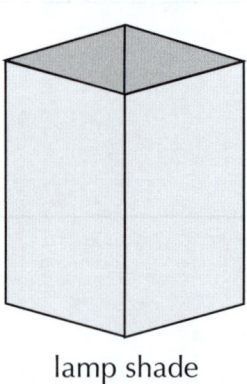

lamp shade

(3 marks)

Section 2 — Graphical Techniques

Drawing Techniques — 4

6 A design for a toaster is shown below.

a) Complete the diagram by naming the **two other views** that are shown in a third angle orthographic projection.

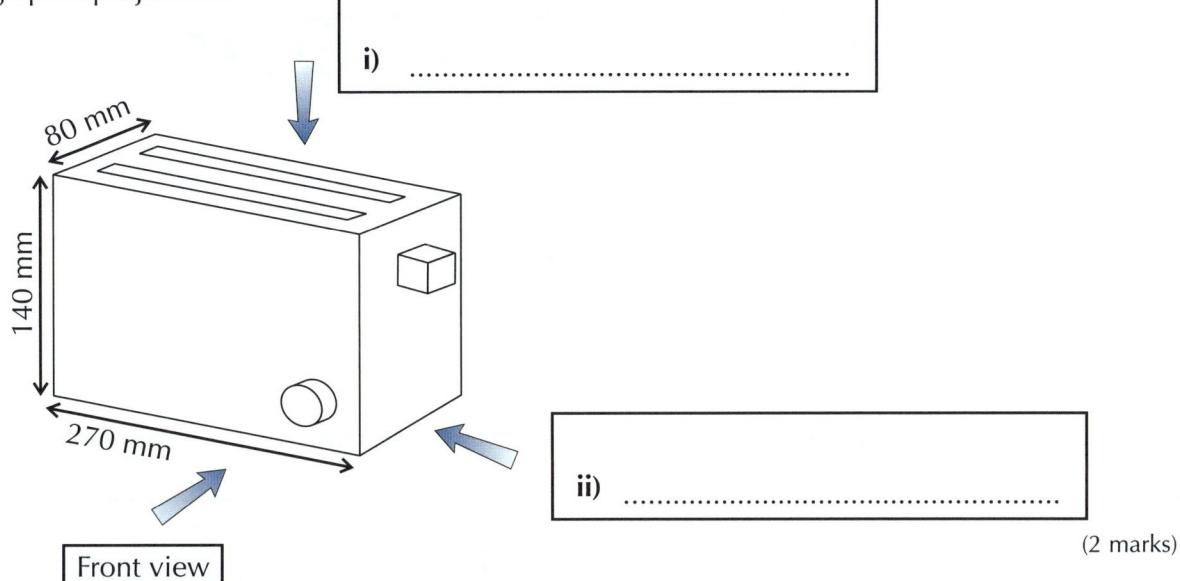

i) ....

ii) ....

Front view

(2 marks)

b) Complete this third angle orthographic projection of the toaster. Include **dimensions** using British Standard conventions.

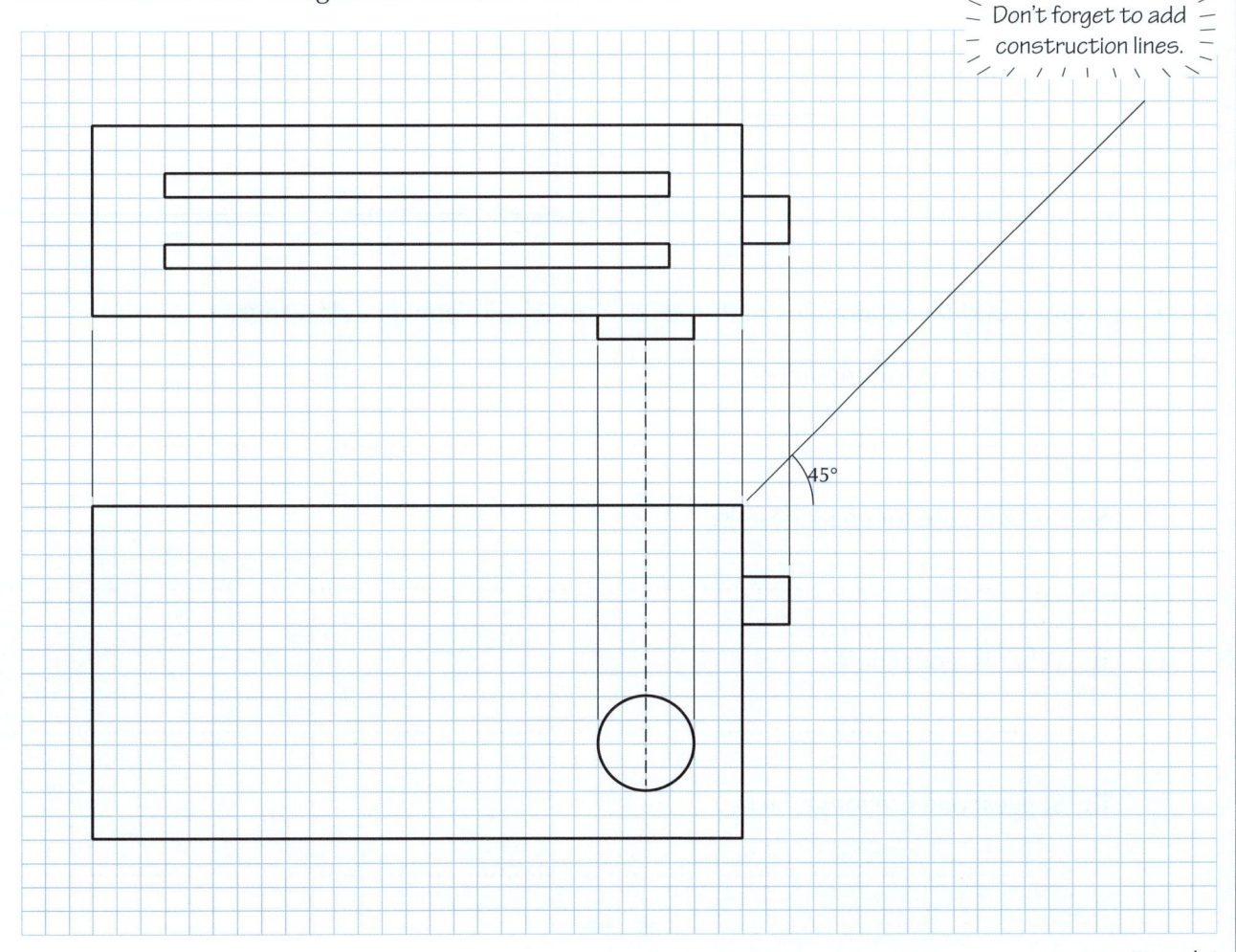

Don't forget to add construction lines.

(3 marks)

Section 2 — Graphical Techniques

Drawing Enhancements — 1

1 Use pencil to **render** this drawing of a camera made from matt plastic, bearing in mind the light source shown.

LIGHT

Render means shading in.

(3 marks)

2 Redraw the bookshelves using the **thick/thin line technique** to make them look solid.

(2 marks)

3 A range of different **drawing materials** can be used to enhance drawings.

a) Suggest **one** use for fine-liners.

....
(1 mark)

b) Suggest **one** use for chalk pastels.

....
(1 mark)

c) i) What is 'gouache'?

....
(1 mark)

ii) Suggest **one** use for gouache.

....
(1 mark)

Section 2 — Graphical Techniques

Drawing Enhancements — 2

4 Colour is a really good way of enhancing drawings.

   a) Explain what complementary colours are.

      ....

      ....
      (2 marks)

   b) **i)** Suggest a contrasting colour to purple.

         ....
         (1 mark)

      ii) Suggest a contrasting colour to green.

         ....
         (1 mark)

5 Explain what is meant by the following terms.

   a) Hue: ....
      (1 mark)

   b) Tone: ....
      (1 mark)

6 A greetings card company want a new design for a **badge** for the front of a child's 5th birthday card.

   Sketch **one** design idea for the badge.
   Use **two** primary colours and **one** secondary colour for the design.

(4 marks)

Section 2 — Graphical Techniques

Presentation Techniques — 1

1 **Render** these drawings to indicate that:

    a) the duck is made of **plastic**   **b)** the spoon is made of **metal**   **c)** the block is made of **wood**

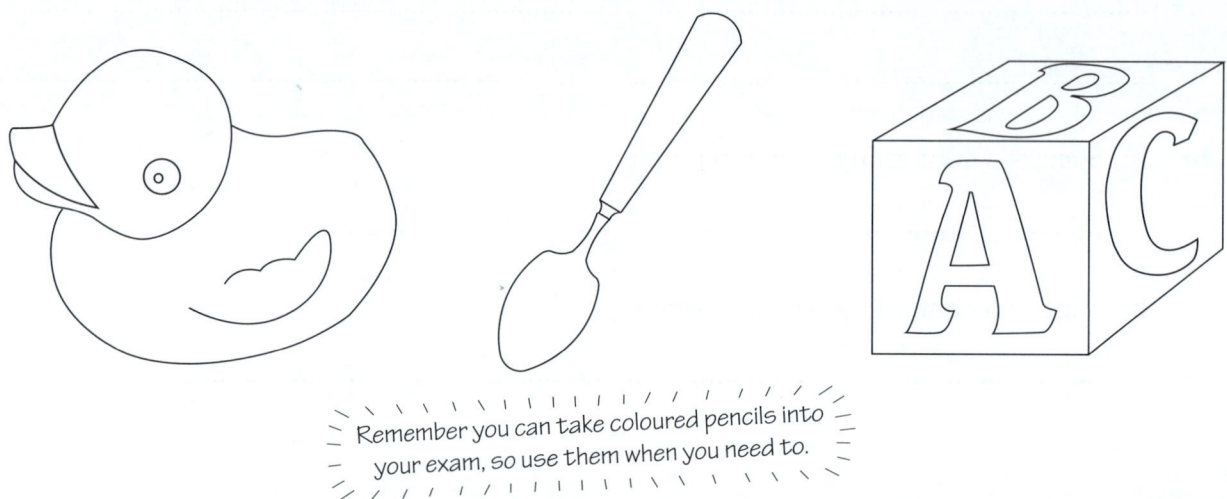

Remember you can take coloured pencils into your exam, so use them when you need to.

(6 marks)

2 A design for a new mobile phone is shown below. The screen will be shiny plastic, the phone itself will be smooth, coloured plastic and the buttons will be silver-coloured metal.

Render the drawing to suggest these materials and add **thick/thin lines** to make the object look more solid. Make sure you take into account the light source shining from the left.

LIGHT

(5 marks)

Section 2 — Graphical Techniques

Presentation Techniques — 2

3 A toy company wants to design a new toy car.

Sketch and annotate **one** design idea. Render it so it looks like the material you would use to make it.

(3 marks)

4 CAD can be used to manipulate and present a design.

Explain the advantages of using CAD in design.

....

....

....
(3 marks)

5 Software can be used for **photo manipulation**.

a) Give **two** examples of photo manipulation software.

1. ....

2. ....
(2 marks)

b) Describe **three** ways that photographs can be changed using photo manipulation software.

1. ....

2. ....

3. ....
(3 marks)

Section 2 — Graphical Techniques

Section Three — Packaging and Marketing

Packaging and the Environment — 1

1 A plastic DVD case is shown in the photos.

Outside — Clear plastic front cover
Inside — Clips, Centre clip for DVD

a) Describe and explain **one** design feature of the case that makes transporting many DVDs easier.

....

....

....
(2 marks)

b) Describe **two features** of the case that allow information about the disk to be displayed.

1. ....

2. ....
(2 marks)

c) Identify **two ways** in which the case protects the disk.

1. ....

2. ....
(2 marks)

2 Crisps lose their flavour and become stale if **not preserved** against contact with air. Two types of packaging for crisps are shown below.

Container 1: Foil pack (Crisps!)

Container 2: Cardboard tube with aluminium lining, Plastic lid, Foil cover

a) Explain why a plain cardboard box is **not** a suitable type of packaging for crisps.

....
(1 mark)

b) Describe and explain **one advantage** and **one disadvantage** of **container 2**.

Advantage: ....

....
(2 marks)

Disadvantage: ....

....
(2 marks)

Section 3 — Packaging and Marketing

Packaging and the Environment — 2

3 Some types of sandwich packaging are made from **non-recyclable, non-biodegradable** plastic.

a) Explain why the sandwich packaging could be considered bad for the environment.

....

....

....

(4 marks)

b) In the space below design a **more environmentally friendly** type of packaging for the sandwich. Use notes to explain the features of your design.

(4 marks)

4 Packaging for most electronic equipment provides **security** and **protection** for the goods it contains.

a) Identify and explain **one** feature of the packaging for electronic goods that could provide **security** against **theft** for the product contained inside.

....

....

(2 marks)

b) Identify and explain **one** feature of the packaging for electronic goods that could provide **protection** against **impacts** for the product contained inside.

....

....

(2 marks)

Section 3 — Packaging and Marketing

Labelling — 1

1 Labels are used to give information about product **safety**.

For **two** of the hazards given below draw an appropriate hazard symbol.

| Explosive | Harmful | Flammable | Environmental hazard |

Hazard 1: ....   Hazard 2: ....

Your diagram doesn't have to be spot on — it just has to be recognisable and neatly drawn.

(1 mark) (1 mark)

2 A company called PodProtectors™ has developed a new range of **crash helmets**.

a) Explain what the letters ™ stand for and why they are used.

....

....
(2 marks)

b) The helmets have labels with symbols on them that give information about the product. Name the following symbols and explain what they mean.

i) Name: ....

Explanation: ....

....
(2 marks)

ii) Name: ....

Explanation: ....

....
(2 marks)

Section 3 — Packaging and Marketing

Labelling — 2

3 Labels often show how to **dispose** of products or packaging.

Explain what **two** of the symbols shown below mean.
Give an example for each of a product which may show the symbol.

Symbol	Explanation	Example
♳ V		
RECY		
♸ PS		
(alu)		
🗑 (crossed out bin)		

(4 marks)

4 For **one** of the products below, suggest **two** types of information that you would expect to find on the product's label.

a) 1. ....
   2. ....
   (2 marks)

b) 1. ....
   2. ....
   (2 marks)

c) 1. ....
   2. ....
   (2 marks)

Section 3 — Packaging and Marketing

Brands and Marketing

1 **Logos** are very good for promoting a product.
Some companies can be recognised by their logo alone.

a) Name a company that can be recognised by their logo alone.

....
(1 mark)

b) In the space below, draw the company logo.

[ ]

(2 marks)

2 **Advertising** is a really important method of marketing.

a) Give **two** examples of different places where companies can advertise.
Explain **one advantage** of advertising in each place.

Place 1: ....

Advantage: ....
(2 marks)

Place 2: ....

Advantage: ....
(2 marks)

b) Explain why companies may pay celebrities to endorse their products.

....
(1 mark)

3 Slop4Mops™ is a company that makes hair gel for **men**.

Suggest **two** ways they could advertise their product to their target group.

1. ....

2. ....
(2 marks)

Section 3 — Packaging and Marketing

Section Four — Materials and Components

Properties of Materials

1 Materials have different **properties** that make them suitable for different products.

Explain what the following words mean.

a) Hardness

....
(1 mark)

b) Plasticity

....
(1 mark)

c) Durability

....
(1 mark)

d) Brittleness

....
(1 mark)

2 Complete the table by suggesting which **property** is most important for each of the following products. Give a reason for each answer. An example has been done for you.

Product	Property	Reason
Scaffolding	Strength	It needs to be strong enough to cope with the weight that's put on it.
Cycle helmet		
Drill bit		
Jumper for a baby		
Packaging for a cake		

(8 marks)

Section 4 — Materials and Components

Paper and Card — 1

1 **Paper** and **card** are made from wood pulp.

   a) Describe the process used to convert wood to pulp.

     ....

     ....

     (2 marks)

   b) Describe the process used to convert the wood pulp to paper.

     ....

     ....

     (2 marks)

2 There are lots of **different types of paper** that are used for different jobs.

   a) In the table below, state **one property** and **one use** of each type of paper.

Type of paper	Property	Use
Layout		
Cartridge		
Grid		

     (6 marks)

   b) A designer wants to make a **copy** of a drawing.

     i) Suggest which type of paper he should use.

      ....

      (1 mark)

     ii) Explain why this type of paper would be the most suitable.

      ....

      (1 mark)

3 A delivery company is choosing a type of board for their **packaging boxes**. They use the boxes to carry and protect boxes, cans or packets that will be put on shop shelves.

   Suggest a type of board they could use for their packaging boxes. Explain your answer.

   Type of Board: ....

   (1 mark)

   Explanation: ....

   ....

   (2 marks)

Section 4 — Materials and Components

Paper and Card — 2

4 A student is looking for different **sizes of paper** to use for her school project.

  a) State the **size** of paper that fits the requirements below.

  i) Half the size of A5: ....
  (1 mark)

  ii) Double the size of A3: ....
  (1 mark)

  b) She finds some paper that is described as 100 gsm. Describe what gsm means.

  ....

  ....
  (2 marks)

5 **Laminating** paper with another material can change its properties.

  a) Suggest a use for paper laminated with aluminium. Explain your answer.

  Use: ....

  Explanation: ....
  (2 marks)

  b) Suggest a composite material suitable for framing a picture. Explain your answer.

  Material: ....

  Explanation: ....
  (2 marks)

  c) In the space below, design a paper drinks container.
  Annotate your diagram to explain the materials used.

  (3 marks)

Section 4 — Materials and Components

Timber — 1

Only do this page if you've studied Timber

1 Wood can be classified as **hardwood** or **softwood**.

Compare softwoods with hardwoods.

....

....

....

(3 marks)

2 Different types of wood have **different properties** which make them suitable for different purposes.

Complete the table below by stating **two** properties of each type of wood.
State whether each type is hardwood or softwood. An example has been done for you.

Type of wood	Properties	Hard or Soft
Mahogany	Easy to work with Expensive	Hard
Teak		
Scots pine		
Ash		

(9 marks)

3 Name a suitable type of wood that could be used to make each of the products below. Give **one** reason for each answer.

a) Name: ....

Reason: ....

....

(2 marks)

b) Name: ....

Reason: ....

....

(2 marks)

Section 4 — Materials and Components

Timber — 2

Only do this page if you've studied Timber

4 Wood can be bought in many different **forms**.

a) Describe what veneers are. State why they are used.

....

....
(2 marks)

b) What are mouldings and what can they be used for?

....

....
(2 marks)

5 **Finishes** improve the durability and appearance of woods.

Name a suitable finish that could be used for each of the following products.
Give an explanation for your answer.

Dining Table

Exterior Door

Dining Table: ....

....
(2 marks)

Exterior Door: ....

....
(2 marks)

6 In the box below, design and annotate an **outdoor** picnic table and bench set.

You'll be given marks for selecting an appropriate material and finish.

(5 marks)

Section 4 — Materials and Components

Manufactured Boards — 1

Only do this page if you've studied Boards

1 **Manufactured board** is used as an alternative to wood.

Name **three** types of manufactured board.

1. ....

2. ....

3. ....

(3 marks)

2 Name a manufactured board that would be suitable for making each of the products below. Give **one** reason for each answer.

a) Name: ....

Reason: ....

....

(2 marks)

b) Name: ....

Reason: ....

....

(2 marks)

Bottom of a draw

3 Products made from manufactured boards often have a **finish** applied to them.

a) Give a reason why products made from manufactured boards are often given a finish.

....

(1 mark)

b) Describe what laminate is.

....

(1 mark)

c) Identify a suitable finish for each of the following products.

i) Plywood flooring: ....

ii) MDF bookshelf: ....

iii) Mahogany-effect chipboard table: ....

(3 marks)

Section 4 — Materials and Components

Manufactured Boards — 2

Only do this page if you've studied Boards

4 MDF is a commonly used manufactured board.

a) What does MDF stand for?

....
(1 mark)

b) Describe how MDF is constructed.

....

....
(2 marks)

c) **Compare** MDF to chipboard.

....

....
(2 marks)

Chipboard butty

5 Complete the table below by giving the **name** of each type of board. Describe the **process** used to make each type of board.

Diagram of board	Name	Process
		....
		....
		....

(9 marks)

Section 4 — Materials and Components

Metals — 1

Only do this page if you've studied Metals

1 Explain what is meant by an alloy and give **one** example of an alloy.

Explanation: ....

Example: ....

(2 marks)

2 Suggest a metal that would be suitable for making each of the products below. Give **two** properties of each metal.

a) Metal: ....

(1 mark)

Properties:

1. ....

2. ....

(2 marks)

b) Metal: ....

(1 mark)

Properties:

1. ....

2. ....

(2 marks)

c) Metal: ....

(1 mark)

Properties:

1. ....

2. ....

(2 marks)

3 Metals are extracted from the earth's crust in the form of **metal ores**.

Describe the process by which metal ores are transformed into metals.

....

....

....

....

(4 marks)

Section 4 — Materials and Components

Metals — 2

Only do this page if you've studied Metals

4 Metals can be heat-treated to change their properties.

Name and describe **two** different heat treatments that can be applied to metals.

1. ....

....
(2 marks)

2. ....

....
(2 marks)

5 Metals can be **coated** in different substances to protect them.

a) Describe the process of plating metal.

....

....

....
(3 marks)

b) Explain why a designer might choose to lacquer their metal product.

....

....
(2 marks)

6 Design a pair of earrings for **teenage girls**.

Annotate your design to explain your choice of material and finish.

Remember to also think about whether your design is aimed at the target group.

(5 marks)

Section 4 — Materials and Components

Plastics — 1

Only do this page if you've studied Plastics

1 All plastics can be divided into one of two types — **thermoplastic** and **thermosetting**.

  a) Explain the difference between thermoplastics and thermosetting plastics.

  ....

  ....
  (2 marks)

  b) Give **one** example of each type of plastic.

  Thermoplastic: ....

  Thermosetting plastic: ....
  (2 marks)

  c) Give **one benefit** of thermoplastics over thermosetting plastics in terms of environmental impact.

  ....
  (1 mark)

2 Suggest a plastic that would be suitable for making each of the products below. Give **one** reason for each answer.

  a) Plastic: ....

  Reason: ....

  ....
  (2 marks)

  b) Plastic: ....

  Reason: ....

  ....
  (2 marks)

3 Plastic has to be **processed** before it can be used.

  a) State the raw material used to make plastic. ....
  (1 mark)

  b) Outline how the raw material is converted to workable plastic.

  ....

  ....

  ....
  (3 marks)

Section 4 — Materials and Components

Plastics — 2

Only do this page if you've studied Plastics

4 Chemicals can be added to plastics to **improve** their properties.

Explain why each chemical is added to plastic.

a) Plasticisers

....

....
(2 marks)

b) Fillers

....

....
(2 marks)

c) Blowing agents

....

....
(2 marks)

5 Plastics can be processed into a range of different **forms**.

Suggest which form of plastic could be used to produce each product below.

a) The window in a sandwich box.

....
(1 mark)

b) The protective packaging in the box around a computer monitor.

....
(1 mark)

6 A designer is making a plastic CD holder.

a) Explain why a protective surface finish is **not** needed on this product.

....

....
(2 marks)

b) Describe how the product could be finished to give it a nice appearance.

....

....
(2 marks)

Section 4 — Materials and Components

Ceramics — 1

Only do this page if you've studied Ceramics

1 Ceramic plates are made using clay.

    a) **i)** Describe how clay can be turned into a hard ceramic plate.

                ....

                ....

                ....
                (3 marks)

       ii) Plates are often finished with a glaze. What is a glaze?

                ....
                (1 mark)

    b) Name **two** different firing methods that can be used to harden ceramics. Describe the **effect** each method has on a ceramic.

        Method 1: ....

        Effect: ....
                (2 marks)

        Method 2: ....

        Effect: ....
                (2 marks)

2 **Complete** the table below by giving the material that each ceramic product is most likely to be made from. Give **two** reasons why the material is suitable for the product. An example has been done for you.

Product	Material	Reasons
Dining plate	Stoneware clay	Better quality than earthenware clays.
		Whitish in colour.
Plant pot		
Ornamental tea pot		
Thrown pot		

(9 marks)

Section 4 — Materials and Components

Ceramics — 2

Only do this page if you've studied Ceramics

3 Some ceramics are made of **non-clay** materials.

a) i) Name the type of ceramic shown in the photograph. State what it is made from.

Name: ....

Made from: ....

....

(2 marks)

ii) Give **one** use of the ceramic shown in the photograph.

....

(1 mark)

b) i) Name **one other non-clay** ceramic. Describe how it is made.

Name: ....

Made by: ....

(2 marks)

ii) Give **one** property and **one** use of the ceramic you have named above.

Property: ....

Use: ....

(2 marks)

4 Ceramics are used in the **electrical industry**.

State **two places** where ceramics are used in the electrical industry.
For each place, explain why ceramics are suitable.

Place 1: ....

Property: ....

....

(2 marks)

Place 2: ....

Property: ....

....

(2 marks)

Section 4 — Materials and Components

Textiles — 1

Only do this page if you've studied Textiles

1 The properties of two **yarns** are given on the right.

Yarn A
Staple fibres
3-ply

Yarn B
Filament fibres
1-ply

a) **Compare** the characteristics you would expect yarn A and yarn B to have.

....

....

....

....

(4 marks)

b) i) **Compare** natural fibres with synthetic fibres.

....

....

....

(3 marks)

ii) Name **one** synthetic fibre. Give the raw material that it is produced from.

Name: ....

Raw material: ....

(2 marks)

2 Fibres can be **woven**, **knitted** or **bonded** to make fabrics.

a) Describe how each type of fabric is made.

i) Woven fabrics: ....

(1 mark)

ii) Knitted fabrics: ....

(1 mark)

iii) Bonded fabrics: ....

(1 mark)

b) Give **one property** of each type of fabric.

i) Woven fabrics: ....

(1 mark)

ii) Knitted fabrics: ....

(1 mark)

iii) Bonded fabrics: ....

(1 mark)

Section 4 — Materials and Components

Textiles — 2

Only do this page if you've studied Textiles

3 Complete the table by suggesting a suitable fabric for each product. Give **two** reasons for each choice.

Product	Fabric	Reasons for fabric choice
A tie		1. .... 2. ....
Tights		1. .... 2. ....
Polo shirt		1. .... 2. ....

(9 marks)

4 Design a piece of clothing suitable for a gymnast.

Annotate your design to explain your choice of fabric.

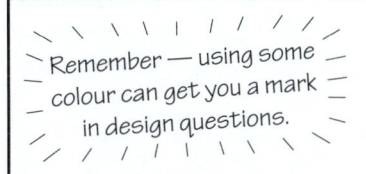

Remember — using some colour can get you a mark in design questions.

(4 marks)

Section 4 — Materials and Components

Textiles — 3

Only do this page if you've studied Textiles

5 Elastane can be combined with cotton to create a **mixed fabric**.

   a) Explain why different fibres are often combined to produce new fabrics.

      ....
(1 mark)

   b) Describe the difference between a blended fabric and a mixed fabric.

      ....

      ....
(2 marks)

6 **Finishes** can improve the performance of fabrics.

   Name **one** suitable finish for each of the following products. Give **one** reason for each choice.

   a) Cotton overalls for a welder: ....

      Reason: ....
(2 marks)

   b) A linen shirt: ....

      Reason: ....
(2 marks)

   c) A nylon tent: ....

      Reason: ....
(2 marks)

7 The Space Coffee Shop is being refurbished.

   In the space below, design a cushion that could be used in the shop. Annotate your design to explain the finish that you have chosen.

The name of the shop should help inspire your design.

(4 marks)

Section 4 — Materials and Components

Food — 1

Only do this page if you've studied Food

1 Food contains many different **nutrients**.

Complete the table by describing why each nutrient is needed by the body. Give **one** food that is high in each nutrient.

Nutrient	Why nutrient is needed	Example food
Starch	It's a source of energy	Potatoes
Protein		
Fat		
Fibre		
Calcium		
Iron		

(10 marks)

2 A company wants to make a **high-energy** snack product that is also **high** in **fibre**.

In the space below, design a suitable snack product for the company. Annotate your design to explain the ingredients you have chosen.

Think about which ingredients are high in energy and fibre.

(4 marks)

Section 4 — Materials and Components

44

Food — 2

Only do this page if you've studied Food

3 Basic food sources are often **processed** before being sold to the consumer.

Name the starting food material for each of the following products. Describe how it is processed.

a) Pork chops

Starting food material: ....

Process: ....

....

....

(4 marks)

b) Flour

Starting food material: ....

Process: ....

....

(3 marks)

c) Butter

Starting food material: ....

Process: ....

....

(3 marks)

4 Food components are available in **different forms**. Two forms are shown below.

A   B

Name each form. Describe **one advantage** and **one disadvantage** of each form.

A: ....

Advantage: ....

Disadvantage: ....

(3 marks)

B: ....

Advantage: ....

Disadvantage: ....

(3 marks)

Section 4 — Materials and Components

Food — 3

Only do this page if you've studied Food

5 Food materials can be **processed** to change their characteristics.

Name the starting material and process used to create each food product.
An example has been done for you.

Food product	Starting material	Process
Shredded carrot	Carrot	Grating
Whipped cream		
Burger		
Chips		

(6 marks)

6 **Combining** ingredients is an essential part of cooking.

a) i) Describe the difference between a solution and a suspension.

....

....

(2 marks)

ii) Give **one** example of a suspension

....

(1 mark)

b) i) Describe what an emulsion is.

....

....

(2 marks)

ii) How can you stop an emulsion from separating?

....

(1 mark)

c) Describe what a gel is.

....

(1 mark)

Section 4 — Materials and Components

Electrical Components — 1

Only do this page if you've studied Electronics

1 **Symbols** are often used to represent electronic **components**.

Complete the table by drawing the component's symbol and describing what it does. An example has been done for you.

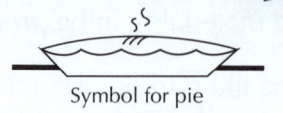

Symbol for pie

Component	Symbol	Description of what it does
Thermistor		Its resistance changes depending on the temperature.
Lamp		
Light-dependent resistor		
Buzzer		
Speaker		

(8 marks)

2 Describe the function of each of the components given below.
Give **one** example of how each component could be used in an electrical circuit.

a) **i)** Resistor: ....

Example: ....

(2 marks)

ii) Capacitor: ....

Example: ....

(2 marks)

b) State the unit that resistance is measured in.

....

(1 mark)

c) What is a farad (F) a unit of measurement for?

....

(1 mark)

d) Name the component shown on the right.
Explain its function in an electrical circuit.

Name: ....

Function: ....

(2 marks)

Section 4 — Materials and Components

Electrical Components — 2

Only do this page if you've studied Electronics

3 A **circuit diagram** is shown below.

a) Explain why the buzzer will **not** sound even though the switch is **closed**.

....

....

....
(2 marks)

b) State **one** property of copper that makes it useful in electrical circuits.

....
(1 mark)

c) Explain the function of a power cell in a circuit.

....

....
(2 marks)

4 Circuits with **specific functions** can be created by combining different electrical components.

a) Design an electrical circuit that will turn a lamp on when a switch is closed.

Remember to include a component that will protect the lamp from high currents.

(3 marks)

b) Suggest **one** product that may use the following electrical components.

i) Light-dependent resistor: ....
(1 mark)

ii) Solenoid: ....
(1 mark)

iii) Buzzer: ....
(1 mark)

Section 4 — Materials and Components

Mechanical Components — 1

Only do this page if you've studied Mechanics

1 In the diagrams below, the **driver gear** is turning **clockwise**.

State which **direction** the **last** driven gear is turning in each diagram.

a) Driver
....
(1 mark)

b) Driver
....
(1 mark)

c) Driver
....
(1 mark)

2 Gears can be used to **change the direction** of motion.

a) Suggest **one** type of gear system that could be used to do this.

....
(1 mark)

b) Draw and annotate a sketch to show how this type of gear system works.

(2 marks)

3 For each gear below, state how many times the driven gear will turn if the driver gear makes **one complete** rotation.

a) Driver — Teeth = 10, Driven — Teeth = 20

....
(1 mark)

b) Driver — Teeth = 20, Driven — Teeth = 10

....
(1 mark)

Section 4 — Materials and Components

Mechanical Components — 2

Only do this page if you've studied Mechanics

3 Name the type of **mechanism** used in the products below.

a) ....
(1 mark)

b) ....
(1 mark)

c) ....
(1 mark)

4 A company has designed a toy crane. The crane uses compressed air and mechanisms to move the arm of the crane and lift loads on the hook.

A
B (uses compressed air)
C

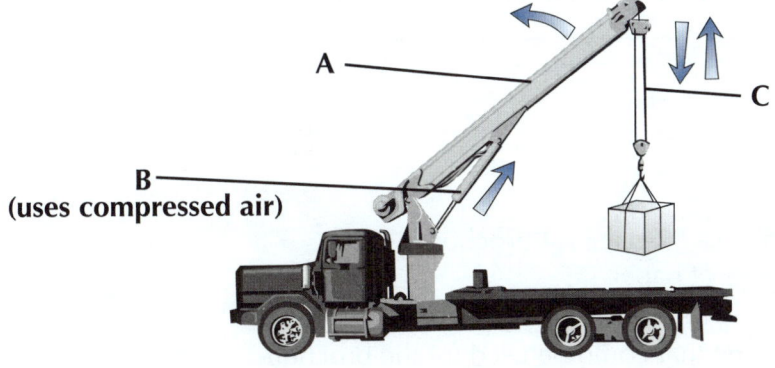

Name **one** of the labelled mechanisms on the toy truck. Draw a diagram to show how the mechanism changes input motion into output motion. Annotate your diagram.

Mechanism: ....

Name: ....

(3 marks)

Section 4 — Materials and Components

Fixings and Bindings

1 The table below shows different types of fixings. State whether each fixing is permanent or temporary, and suggest **one** purpose it might be used for.

Fixing	Permanent or temporary	Purpose
(paperclip)	....	....
(drawing pin)	....	....
(staple)	....	....
(tacks)	....	....

(8 marks)

2 A company wants to make a 12-page A4 brochure by **binding** together sheets of paper.

a) Name a method of binding that could be used for the brochure.

....
(1 mark)

b) Describe how the brochure would be bound using this method.

....

....
(2 marks)

c) Give **two advantages** of this type of binding.

1. ....

2. ....
(2 marks)

Section 4 — Materials and Components

Standard Components

1 **Standard components** are pre-manufactured parts.

Give **three** benefits of using standard components in the manufacturing process.

1. ....

2. ....

3. ....

(3 marks)

2 Many industries use standard components.

Choose **two** of the products from the box.
Suggest **two** standard components that could be used for each product.

| Jeans | Pizza | Magazine | Car | Bookcase |

Product	Standard Component
....	....
....	....

(4 marks)

3 Company A makes individual wedding cakes without using standard components. Company B mass produces cupcakes using standard components such as ready-made icing and cake mixes.

Give **one advantage** and **one disadvantage** of the method used by each company.

a) Company A

Advantage: ....

Disadvantage: ....

(2 marks)

b) Company B

Advantage: ....

Disadvantage: ....

(2 marks)

Section 4 — Materials and Components

New Materials — 1

1 Precious metal clay is an example of a **new material**.

a) What is precious metal clay?

....

....

(2 marks)

b) Give **one** benefit of using precious metal clay instead of other metals.

....

(1 mark)

2 Quantum tunnelling composite is a **smart material**.

a) What are 'smart' materials?

....

(1 mark)

b) Describe what a quantum tunnelling composite is.

....

....

(2 marks)

c) Suggest **one** use of quantum tunnelling composite.

....

(1 mark)

3 Product designers use new materials in modern product design.

Complete the table to give **one** use and **two** properties for each of the following new materials.

Material	Use	Property
Cornstarch Polymers		1. .... 2. ....
Thermochromic Materials		1. .... 2. ....
Shape memory alloys		1. .... 2. ....

(9 marks)

Section 4 — Materials and Components

New Materials — 2

4 **Nanomaterials** have properties which make them useful for manufacturers.

  a) Explain what nanomaterials are.

  ....

  ....
  (2 marks)

  b) Explain how nanomaterials could be used to improve the properties of **one** of these products.

  Medical Dressing ....

  ....

  Glass windows ....

  ....

  Sports kit ....

  ....
  (2 marks)

5 **Integrated electronics** is often used in product design.

  a) Describe what is meant by the term 'integrated electronics'.

  ....
  (1 mark)

  b) Suggest **one** use of integrated electronics in product design.

  ....
  (1 mark)

6 Design a children's toy that uses new materials, smart materials or nanomaterials in its production. Annotate your design and explain your choices.

[blank box for design]

(4 marks)

Section 4 — Materials and Components

Section Five — Social and Environmental Issues

Safety — 1

1 **Safety** is vital when designing and manufacturing a product.

   a) Suggest **two** safety rules you should follow when using tools and machinery.

      1. ....

      2. ....
                                                                                           (2 marks)

   b) Suggest **one** safety rule you should follow when handling materials and waste.

      ....
                                                                                           (1 mark)

2 For **one** of the following pieces of safety equipment give an example of when it might be used and explain why it is needed.

Safety goggles ....

....

....

Protective gloves ....

....

....

An apron ....

....

....
                                                                                           (2 marks)

3 **Risk assessments** should always be carried out before making a product.

   a) What is a risk assessment?

      ....

      ....
                                                                                          (2 marks)

   b) Identify a hazard associated with the use of **one** of the following materials.

      Fresh meat: ....

      A large piece of metal: ....

      Stuffing made from very fine fibres: ....
                                                                                          (1 mark)

Section 5 — Social and Environmental Issues

Safety — 2

4 Risk assessments should include all **equipment** to be used during manufacturing.

Select **two** pieces of equipment from the box below. Identify **one** hazard of using each piece of equipment and suggest a suitable precaution to follow when using it.

soldering iron   strip heater   food mixer   guillotine   sewing machine   craft knife

Equipment 1: ....

Hazard: ....

Precaution: ....
(2 marks)

Equipment 2: ....

Hazard: ....

Precaution: ....
(2 marks)

5 A castle is celebrating its 300th birthday by making and selling the products shown below.

Cake   Plastic toy   Teddy

Answer the following questions for **one** of the products. Circle the product you have chosen.

a) Describe **two** hazards that might occur when making the product.

1. ....

2. ....
(2 marks)

b) Suggest **one** way the **designer** could make sure the product is safe for the consumer.

....
(1 mark)

c) Suggest **one** way the **manufacturer** could make sure the product is safe for the consumer.

....
(1 mark)

Section 5 — Social and Environmental Issues

Quality — 1

1 A product's **quality** can be judged by many different criteria. Two bikes are shown below.

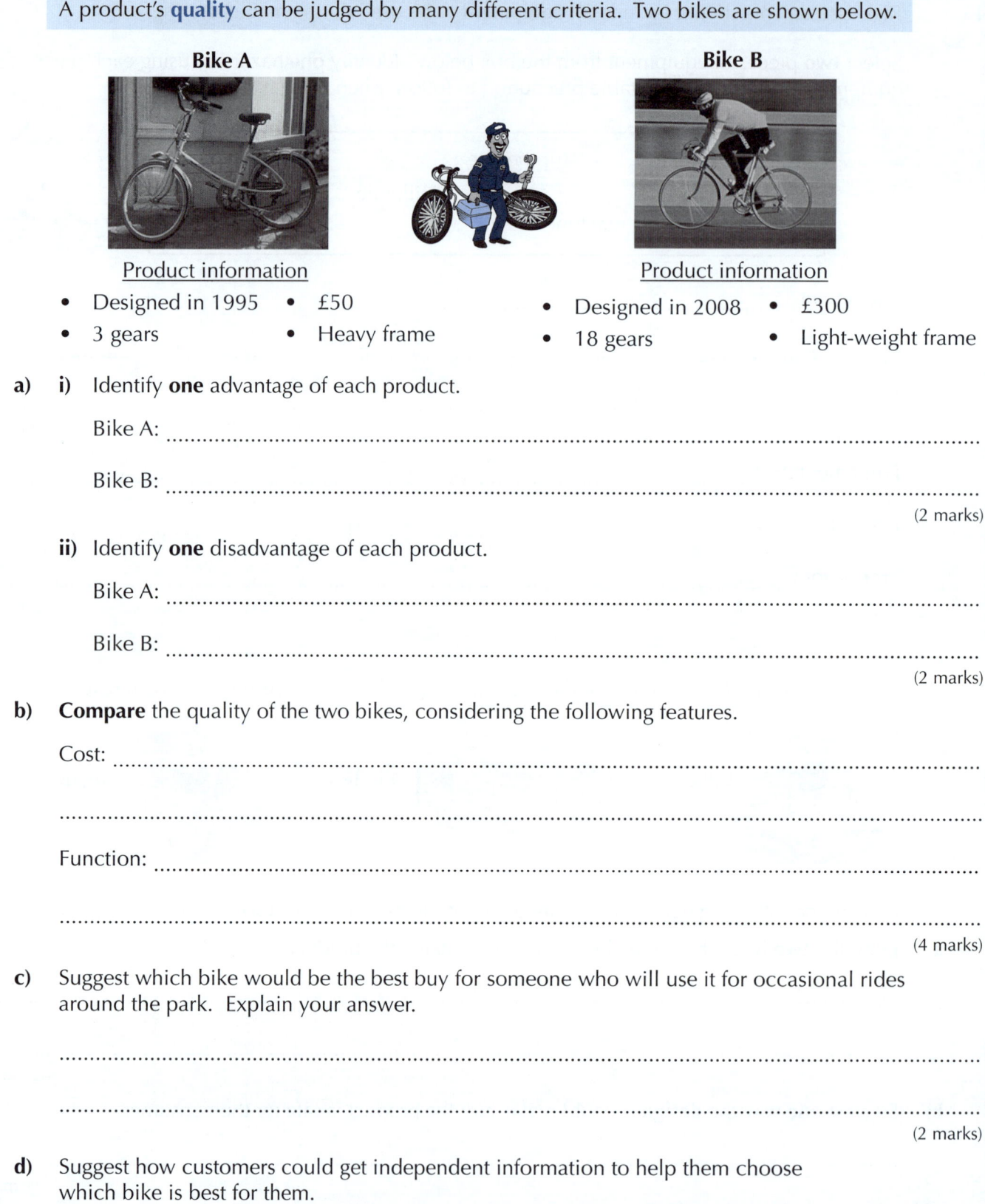

Bike A

Bike B

Product information
- Designed in 1995
- 3 gears
- £50
- Heavy frame

Product information
- Designed in 2008
- 18 gears
- £300
- Light-weight frame

a) **i)** Identify **one** advantage of each product.

Bike A: ....

Bike B: ....
(2 marks)

ii) Identify **one** disadvantage of each product.

Bike A: ....

Bike B: ....
(2 marks)

b) **Compare** the quality of the two bikes, considering the following features.

Cost: ....

....

Function: ....

....
(4 marks)

c) Suggest which bike would be the best buy for someone who will use it for occasional rides around the park. Explain your answer.

....

....
(2 marks)

d) Suggest how customers could get independent information to help them choose which bike is best for them.

....

....
(2 marks)

Section 5 — Social and Environmental Issues

Quality — 2

2 There are **consumer laws** that help protect customers from unsafe and unreliable products.

Name **two** consumer laws that manufacturers must obey and describe what each law does.

Law 1
Name: ....

Description: ....
(2 marks)

Law 2
Name: ....

Description: ....
(2 marks)

3 **Quality control** is an important part of the manufacturing process.

a) **i)** What does quality control involve?

....

....
(2 marks)

ii) Give **one** example of a quality control check for a birthday card.

....
(1 mark)

b) Give **two** reasons why manufacturers have quality checks for their products.

1. ....

2. ....
(2 marks)

c) Some manufacturers have **quality circles** at their factories.
Explain what a quality circle is.

....

....
(2 marks)

4 Describe three **quality control tests** you might carry out on a roll of kitchen towel.

1. ....

2. ....

3. ....
(3 marks)

Section 5 — Social and Environmental Issues

Ethics and Environmental Issues — 1

1 All products have a **carbon footprint**.

a) Explain why all products have a carbon footprint.

....

....
(2 marks)

b) The size of a product's carbon footprint is affected by its product miles.
Explain what is meant by the term 'product miles'.

....
(1 mark)

2 Some products are advertised as **'fair trade'**.

Explain what 'fair trade' means.

....

....

....
(3 marks)

3 It's really important to think about the **6 Rs** when designing a product.

Complete the table below so that each row contains a **6 R word**, an **explanation** of the word and an **example** of how the word could be taken into account when making a product.
An example has been done for you.

6 R word	Explanation	Example
Repair	It's better to fix things than throw them away	Provide spare buttons with a cardigan
Rethink		
	You should reduce the impact the product has on the environment	
		Make the product from recycled material

(6 marks)

Section 5 — Social and Environmental Issues

Ethics and Environmental Issues — 2

4 Soup can be sold in a variety of **packaging types**, for example in tins or cartons.

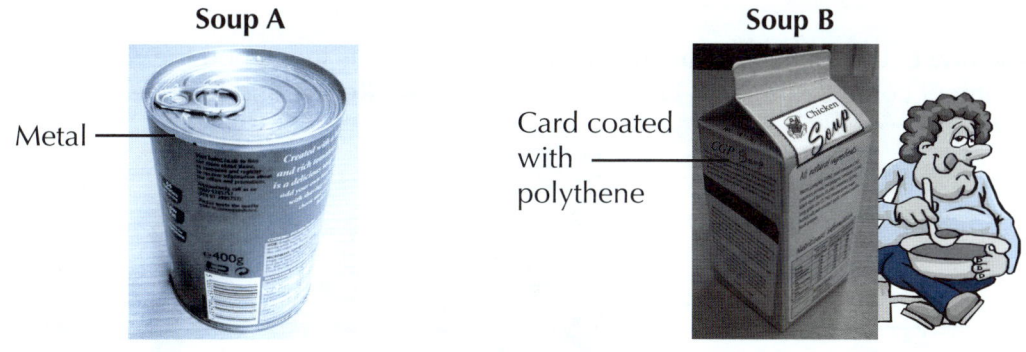

Soup A — Metal

Soup B — Card coated with polythene

a) **Compare** how environmentally friendly the two types of packaging are.

....

....

....
(3 marks)

b) Give **one advantage** of using recycled materials for a product or its packaging.

....
(1 mark)

c) Give **two problems** associated with recycling.

1. ....

2. ....
(2 marks)

5 The packaging of Tuts Chocolate Treats has been changed to make it more **environmentally friendly**.

Old — clear plastic window, cardboard — Tuts Chocolate Treats 250g

New — cardboard — Tuts Chocolate Treats 250g

Explain why the **new** packaging might be regarded as more environmentally friendly.

....

....

....
(3 marks)

Section 5 — Social and Environmental Issues

Ethics and Environmental Issues — 3

6 The **design**, **manufacture** and **disposal** of products should have as little impact on the environment as possible.

Choose **one** of the products shown below. Explain how its impact on the environment could be limited. Use the ideas of **Reuse**, **Refuse** and **Reduce**.

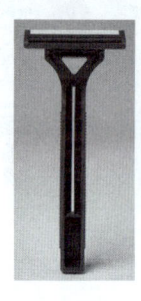

Disposable plastic razor

Teddy bear

Cranberry juice and carton

Reuse: ....

....
(2 marks)

Refuse: ....

....
(2 marks)

Reduce: ....

....
(2 marks)

7 Convenience foods and snacks are popular lunchtime purchases.

In the space below, design some packaging for an apple-flavoured snack bar for children. Annotate your sketch to show how the packaging is environmentally friendly.

Think about the 6 Rs if you're struggling.

(4 marks)

Section 5 — Social and Environmental Issues

Section Six — Processes and Manufacture

Tools — 1

1 Name **one** of the following tools and describe a process that you would use it for.

a)

Name: ....
(1 mark)

Process: ....

....
(1 mark)

b)

Name: ....
(1 mark)

Process: ....

....
(1 mark)

c)

Name: ....
(1 mark)

Process: ....

....
(1 mark)

d)

Name: ....
(1 mark)

Process: ....

....
(1 mark)

e)

Name: ....
(1 mark)

Process: ....

....
(1 mark)

Section 6 — Processes and Manufacture

Tools — 2

2 Name a **machine tool** that could be used to carry out the following processes.

a) Make a curved cut in MDF:

Machine tool:

....

(1 mark)

b) Turn and shape a piece of wood:

Machine tool:

....

(1 mark)

c) Sharpen a chisel blade.

Machine tool: ....

(1 mark)

3 A piece of mild **steel** 4 mm thick needs a hole adding to it.

a) Suggest a suitable machine tool to use to make the hole

....

(1 mark)

b) Suggest a suitable drill bit to use to make the hole

....

(1 mark)

4 A manufacturer has been asked to make the piston head shown on the right.

Describe the machine tools and processes that would be used to make the piston head from an aluminium round bar of 60 mm diameter and 150 mm length.

....

....

....

....

(3 marks)

Section 6 — Processes and Manufacture

Forming and Bending — 1

1 An **anvil** is used in bending and shaping some metals.

   a) Name **one** metal that is often shaped using an anvil.

....
(1 mark)

   b) Describe the process by which metal is formed into shape using an anvil.

....

....

....
(3 marks)

2 The bracket shown below is made from 5 mm thick **mild steel**.

   a) Describe how you would prepare a flat piece of metal so it is ready for bending.

....

....
(2 marks)

   b) Draw a diagram to show how you would make the bend in the bracket.
      Name any equipment you would use.

(2 marks)

Section 6 — Processes and Manufacture

Forming and Bending — 2

3 The book end shown on the right is made using **acrylic**.

  a) Suggest **one** piece of equipment that could be used to bend the acrylic.

  ....
  (1 mark)

  b) Describe the process used to bend the acrylic.

  ....

  ....

  ....
  (3 marks)

4 A design for a **wooden** rocking chair is shown on the right.

  The rockers are made from strips of laminated wood.

  a) Explain what laminated wood is.

  ....

  ....
  (1 mark)

  b) Use notes and sketches to show clearly how you would make the rockers in a school workshop.

  (5 marks)

Section 6 — Processes and Manufacture

Casting and Moulding — 1

1 Using notes and sketches, show how a plastic bottle can be made using **blow moulding**.

(3 marks)

2 Suggest **one** suitable manufacturing process for each of the following products.

a) A key:

....
(1 mark)

b) Aluminium bannister rails:

....
(1 mark)

c) A plastic bucket:

....
(1 mark)

3 Draw a diagram to show how **extrusion** is carried out. Add labels and notes where necessary.

(4 marks)

Section 6 — Processes and Manufacture

Casting and Moulding — 2

4 Some manufacturing processes **mould** materials.

Describe each of the processes used for moulding given below.

   a) Vacuum forming:

....

....

....
(3 marks)

   b) Die casting:

....

....

....
(3 marks)

   c) Injection moulding:

....

....

....
(3 marks)

5 Suggest whether each product below was made by vacuum forming, die casting or injection moulding.

   a) Metal toy car: ....
(1 mark)

   b) A plastic mask: ....
(1 mark)

   c) A plastic box: ....
(1 mark)

Section 6 — Processes and Manufacture

Scale of Production — 1

1 Products can be manufactured using **one-off**, **batch** or **mass** production.

Describe each of these production methods.
Give **one** example of a product each method is commonly used to make.

One-off production: ....

....

Example: ....
(3 marks)

Batch production: ....

....

Example: ....
(3 marks)

Mass production: ....

....

Example: ....
(3 marks)

2 For **two** of the products given below, suggest whether they are likely to be made by one-off, batch or mass production. Explain your answers.

| Soup for a dinner party | Personalised invitations for a birthday party | An individually-designed wedding dress | A Formula 1™ car |
| Tinned soup | Birthday party invitations sold in a supermarket | Jeans to be sold in a high street shop | A 4-door family car |

Product 1: ....

Method of production: ....

Reason: ....
(2 marks)

Product 2: ....

Method of production: ....

Reason: ....
(2 marks)

Section 6 — Processes and Manufacture

Scale of Production — 2

3 Some companies use **continuous production** to make their goods.

   a) Describe what continuous production is and why it is used.

....

....

(2 marks)

   b) Suggest **two** products that could be made using continuous production.

      1. ....

      2. ....

(2 marks)

4 Some manufacturers use a **just-in-time** (JIT) system.

   a) Describe how a JIT system works.

....

....

(2 marks)

   b) Give **two advantages** of using a JIT system.

      1. ....

      2. ....

(2 marks)

   c) Describe **one risk** of using a JIT system.

....

(1 mark)

5 The scale of production of a product can affect its **design**.

Choose **one** of the products given below. Suggest how making one, 300 and 10 000 of the product would affect its design. Circle the product you have chosen.

| Birthday cake | Formal shoes | Earrings |

   a) One: ....

....

(2 marks)

   b) 300: ....

....

(2 marks)

   c) 10 000: ....

....

(2 marks)

Section 6 — Processes and Manufacture

Manufacturing Systems and ICT — 1

1 Manufacturing systems are made up of **inputs**, **processes** and **outputs**.

For **two** of the following output products, fill in **one** missing input and outline the process used to make the product. An example has been done for you.

INPUT	PROCESS	OUTPUT
Wood	Cut pieces of wood to size. Assemble pieces of wood.	Wooden table
		Silk cushion
		Muffin
		Business card
		Mug

(6 marks)

2 A designer is making some 'no dogs allowed' signs. She wants to paint a logo onto MDF before applying stick-on lettering and finally attaching the signs to poles so they will stand up. Draw a **flow chart** to show this process. Include a **feedback loop** to show a quality check.

Think about the order it would be made in before you start drawing.

(5 marks)

Section 6 — Processes and Manufacture

Manufacturing Systems and ICT — 2

3 **Video conferencing** is used by some manufacturers.

   a) What is video conferencing?

   ....
   (1 mark)

   b) Explain why manufacturers might want to use video conferencing.

   ....

   ....
   (2 marks)

4 For each of the following uses of **ICT**, describe what they are and explain why a manufacturer might choose to use them.

   a) Software sharing

   ....

   ....
   (2 marks)

   b) Data transfer

   ....

   ....
   (2 marks)

   c) Stock control

   ....

   ....
   (2 marks)

5 A UK design company is producing a birthday card that is going to be manufactured in a factory in China using a JIT process.

   Describe how ICT could be used in the design and manufacture of this product.

   a) Design

   ....

   ....
   (2 marks)

   b) Manufacture

   ....

   ....
   (2 marks)

Section 6 — Processes and Manufacture

Manufacturing Systems — 1

1 There are a number of features that help a manufacturing system run **efficiently**.

Describe how each of the features below should work in order for a system to run smoothly and efficiently.

a) **i)** The workforce

....

....
(2 marks)

ii) Tools, equipment and materials

....

....
(2 marks)

b) Suggest **three** other features that would help improve the efficiency of a manufacturing system.

1. ....

2. ....

3. ....
(3 marks)

2 Lots of kitchens are designed to have a **working triangle**.

a) Explain what is meant by a working triangle.

....

....
(2 marks)

b) In the space below, roughly sketch a kitchen clearly highlighting the working triangle.

(2 marks)

Section 6 — Processes and Manufacture

Manufacturing Systems — 2

3 A company is setting up a manufacturing workplace for making paper bun cases.

Draw a diagram to show the most efficient layout for the workplace.
Include all the work stations given below.

Work stations:
(not in correct order)

| Packing area | Finishing | Dispatch area |
| Cutting machine | Folding | Raw material storage |

Start by thinking about the order of production.

Loading/ unloading bay

(3 marks)

4 The **layout** of equipment and materials in a workplace helps ensure quality and efficiency of manufacture. It is also important for safety reasons.

Describe **one** of the following common workplace features. Explain how it affects production.

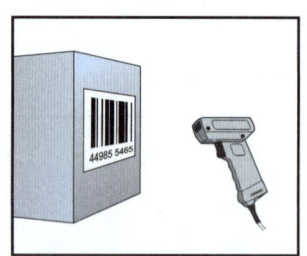

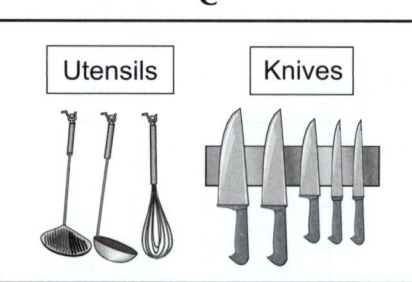

A   B   C

Chosen feature: ....

Description: ....

Explanation: ....

....

(2 marks)

Section 6 — Processes and Manufacture

CAD/CAM — 1

1 CAD and CAM are important parts of the design process for some products.

   a) **i)** What does CAD stand for?

   ....
   (1 mark)

   ii) Explain why CAD is used in the design process.

   ....

   ....
   (2 marks)

   b) **i)** What does CAM stand for?

   ....
   (1 mark)

   ii) Explain how CAM is used in the manufacturing process.

   ....

   ....
   (2 marks)

   iii) Give **one** example of a CAM machine. Explain what it is used for.

   Example: ....

   Use: ....
   (2 marks)

2 CAD and CAM are used in the design and manufacture of a wide range of products.

   Name a product of your choice. Explain how CAD and CAM can be used in its production.

   Product: ....

   Use of CAD: ....

   ....

   ....
   (2 marks)

   Use of CAM: ....

   ....

   ....
   (2 marks)

Section 6 — Processes and Manufacture

CAD/CAM — 2

3 CAM machines can be **2-axis** or **3-axis** machines.

Explain the difference between a 2-axis and a 3-axis CAM machine.

....

....

....
(2 marks)

4 For **three** of the following products, give an example of a CAM machine that could be used to produce it.

a) sandwich box net

....

b) plastic prototype mouse

....

c) poster design

....

d) cardboard stencil

....

e) engraved metal sign

....

f) stair spindle

....
(3 marks)

5 Explain the **advantages** of using CAD and CAM when designing and making products.

....

....

....

....
(4 marks)

Section 6 — Processes and Manufacture

Consistency of Production — 1

1 A prototype birthday card has been made by sticking **identical** balloon and candle shapes on top of each other to give a 3D effect. The card is shown on the right.

In the space below, sketch **one** template that could be used to make a batch of 200 cards more quickly.

Use annotated diagrams to show how the template would be used and what it would be made of.

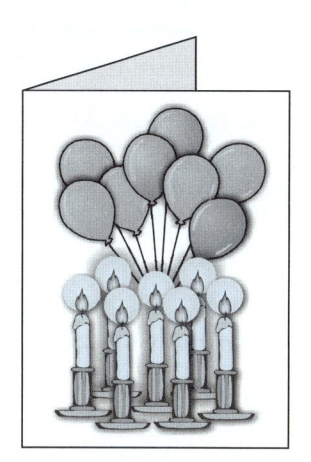

You need at least two diagrams — one of the template and one showing how the template should be used.

(5 marks)

2 A company is producing a batch of shelving units using a **jig**.

a) Describe what a jig does.

....
(1 mark)

b) List **two** advantages of using a jig.

1. ....

2. ....
(2 marks)

Section 6 — Processes and Manufacture

Consistency of Production — 2

3 **Moulds** are used to reproduce 3D shapes.

   a) Name **two** processes that moulds are used in.

      1. ....

      2. ....
                                                                                                                     (2 marks)

   b) Give **two advantages** and **two disadvantages** of using moulds.

      Advantages: ....

      ....
                                                                                                                      (2 marks)

      Disadvantages: ....

      ....
                                                                                                                      (2 marks)

4 A **prototype** free standing table menu is shown on the right.

The prototype was first drawn on paper, then cut out by hand using scissors. It was then folded to form the menu. The measurements were found to be incorrect and the menu had a poor finish with ugly rough edges.

   a) Explain how CAD could be used to make a more accurate prototype.

      ....

      ....

      ....

      ....
                                                                                                                      (4 marks)

   b) Explain why CAM would be useful for accurately manufacturing a batch of the table menus.

      ....

      ....

      ....
                                                                                                                      (3 marks)

   c) Suggest a CAM machine that could be used to make the menus.

      ....
                                                                                                                      (1 mark)

Section 6 — Processes and Manufacture